A VICTORIAN VILLAGE

Martin Parsons

Wayland

First published in 1995 by Wayland (Publishers) Ltd
61 Western Road, Hove, East Sussex, BN3 1JD

Editor: Sarah Doughty
Concept design: Derek Lee
Book design: Pardoe Blacker Ltd

British Library Cataloguing in Publication Data
Parsons, Martin
A Victorian Village
I. Title
942.009734

ISBN 0-7502-1398-1

Printed and bound by B.P.C Paulton Books Ltd

Picture acknowledgements

Archie Miles 33 bottom; The Billie Love Historical Collection 12, 12-13, 30, 35; The Bridgeman Art Library 38; Peter Cox, Fotosparks, Reading 7, 8, 13 top, 17 both, 18 and *front cover*, 19 bottom, 21, 27, 32 top, 42 top right & left, bottom centre & right, 43 top right & bottom right and left, *back cover* bottom; E.T. Archive 14, 37 bottom, 39 top; Eye Ubiquitous 28 (Michael Reed), 34 bottom (D. Gill); Hulton Deutsch 24, Mary Evans Picture Library 15 top, 20, 31; National Museum of Wales 33 top; Norfolk Museums Service (Gressenhall) 26; Martin Parsons *title page*, 37 top, 42 bottom left, 43 top left; Desmond Maurice Redgrave 36; Rural History Centre, University of Reading 29, 39 bottom; Mr and Mrs D. N. Stanbrook 4 and *front cover*, 6, 15 bottom, 16 and *front cover*, 19 top, 25, 32 bottom, 34 top, *back cover* top; Wayland Picture Library 22, 23, 44 top, 45; Richard Wood 44 bottom. The illustrations on pages 10-11 and 42-43 were supplied by John Yates.

Contents

Introduction

This book investigates the local history of a rural village in Victorian times (1837-1901). Local history is the study of the area where you live – your home town or village. To find out about an area, a historian can use a variety of local sources, such as written documents, photographs, buildings and artefacts.

By studying the village of Bradfield you will learn how to find and use evidence from similar sources so that you can investigate a local area for yourself.

Primary evidence is used throughout this book. Primary sources are those that are in their original form and have not been changed. For example, if you kept a

A Victorian family at Home Farm in Bradfield. The head of the family is called Henry Smith.

The census of 1891 of the parish of Bradfield tells us a great deal about the people who lived in the village. This simplified extract is for a house in Southend Road.

Civic Parish Bradfield

Road or street name	Name and Surname		Relation to head of family	Age	Profession or occupation	Where born
3. Southend Road	George Millson		Head; widower	45	Bricklayer	Berks. Stanford Dingley
	Alice J.	Do.	Daughter	17	Housekeeper	Do.
	Ellen L.	Do.	Daughter	15		Do.
	George J.	Do.	Son	14	Farm labourer	Do.
	Sarah A.	Do.	Daughter	12	Scholar	Do.
	Lizzie E.	Do.	Daughter	10	Scholar	Do.
	Ruth L.	Do.	Daughter	3		Do.
	Esther M.	Do.	Daughter	3		Do.

diary and used some of the information from it in a school project, you would be using primary evidence. A census is a type of primary evidence that can tell us many things about a local area. Since 1801, detailed questionnaires have been sent to every household in Britain once every ten years. The householder completes the form and the information from it is then sorted and stored. The public can look at the information after one hundred years. Today, people can look at the 1891 census, but no one will be able to see the 1901 census until 2001.

The census for an area can be seen at a County Record Office or a large central reference library. The details on the census can be very useful in finding out who lived in a certain village, town, street or house, the jobs they did, where they came from and the number of people in their family. For example, if you look at the extract from the 1891 census of Bradfield you will be able to see that George Millson, a 45-year-old bricklayer, lived in Southend Road with his six daughters and son. He was born in Stanford Dingley, a village 5 km away. We also know that his wife had died because he is listed as 'widower'. You can see more of the census in the Appendix on page 40.

School Lane in Bradfield in Victorian times.

Another source of information we can use to find out about a village is a school log-book. You will find extracts from a log-book in the chapter about the village school. The head teacher in your school has to write down in the school log-book all the events, special holidays, punishments given and all other things that affect the school, including bad weather or anything else that may cause the school to be closed.

By examining a log-book from the Victorian period, a historian can get a good idea of what went on in the school and also what happened in the local community. The log-books from small village schools are especially important because some head teachers wrote in great detail and described events that took place throughout the year within the area.

Photographs are also primary sources and can be very useful for two reasons. They show what was happening at the time the picture was taken. This is called the witting testimony. But they also show other things that the photographer did not take deliberately but are part of the photograph. This information is called the unwitting testimony and is

School Lane, renamed Cock Lane, today.

often more useful than witting testimony. Look at the picture of the Smith family on page 4. You can see the fashions middle-class Victorians were wearing. Other photographs can also show what the weather was like at the time, the type of transport that was used, the style of streetlights in the background, and so on.

Look at the photograph of School Lane on page 6. The photographer took the picture to show the houses and the people standing in the road. This is the witting testimony. But there is unwitting testimony as well. You can also see their style of dress and that the man is carrying a gun, something which would not happen today. This may give us an idea as to what job he did, or perhaps he had just been out shooting to get food for the pot. We cannot tell from the picture alone. We would have to support this idea by using other evidence.

It is interesting to compare historical photographs with ones taken in the same place today. If you look at the modern photograph of School Lane (which has been renamed Cock Lane) you will notice that the entrance posts have been replaced. But all the houses on the left have remained almost the same.

Origins

Many villages have long histories and the clue to their origin can often be found in their name. If you can find the original spelling of a settlement, you will have a good idea of how old it is because the way the name is spelt can help you date its beginnings.

Throughout the early history of Britain, people came from other areas of northern Europe and settled in various parts of the country. These people all had different languages and their own names for farms, homesteads and other features of the land. Many of these names are still

The area of the old mill in Bradfield, the origin of the village.

Invaders	Clues	Reason	Examples
Roman	Caster, Cester Chester	Many of their first settlements were army encampments. The Latin for camp is 'caster' or 'castra'.	Cirencester Colchester Silchester
Saxon	-tun, -ton, -wich ham, wick meaning 'farm' -hamm meaning 'meadow' -ley, -leigh meaning 'clearing' -burgh meaning 'fortified place'	Saxons were more concerned with farming than fighting, so most of their names have something to do with agriculture.	Kingston (king's farm) Shepton (sheep farm) Alnwick (farm by the River Aln) Cowley (cow pasture) Edinburgh (Edwin's fort)
Viking	-thorpe meaning 'small hamlet' -by meaning 'homestead' -borough meaning 'fort'	Vikings built forts to attack the Saxons. But they also settled and left the names of these settlements.	Middlesborough

with us today, although some have been changed slightly. If you look at the chart above, you can see some examples of settlements from history.

Some places are not linked to any group of people but get their name from the type of work that was going on in or around the village. Most of these names had something to do with the land; for instance, Kingswood means 'the wood belonging to the king', and Abbeytown means 'the town near the Abbey'. Other places got their names from a particular feature of the land to form names such as Ox*ford*, Cam*bridge* or Avon*mouth*.

The name of the village of Bradfield simply means 'broad field'. This tells us that its origin must have been something to do with farming. Bradfield is still a rural settlement, about 60 km west of London in the county of Berkshire. The modern settlement is made up of two villages – Bradfield, the original village site around the mill and the River Pang; and Southend Bradfield, which developed along a ridge of a hill, forming a communication link with the west.

Development of a village

A. Village (e.g. Fordcombe) grew up around a village green

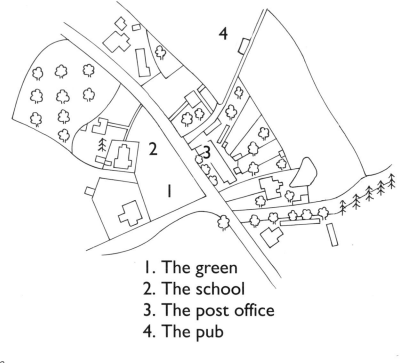

1. The green
2. The school
3. The post office
4. The pub

B. Village (e.g. Aberfan) grew up along a road

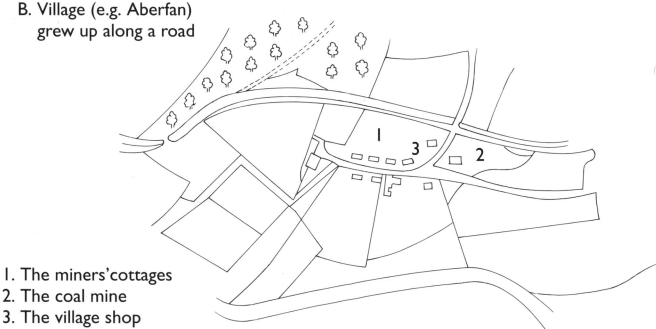

1. The miners' cottages
2. The coal mine
3. The village shop

These illustrations show how some villages have developed.

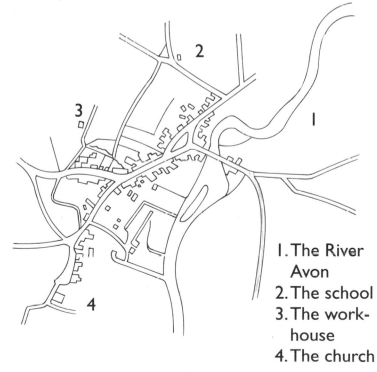

C. Village (e.g. Avonmouth) grew up at the mouth of a river

1. The dock
2. The smithy
3. The lighthouse
4. The River Avon

D. Village (e.g. Fordingbridge) grew up at the lowest bridging point of a river

1. The River Avon
2. The school
3. The workhouse
4. The church

The shape of a village usually develops over a long period of time. Its growth is affected by activities such as fishing, mining, quarrying or factory working. Industry grew enormously in Victorian times. Small communities became towns and cities because they had natural resources such as iron ore, or a source of power such as water or coal. Villages that were unaffected by industrialization, such as fishing villages in Cornwall, remained almost the same as they had been for centuries.

Villages developed their shapes in different ways. They may have developed around a village green, around a specific building such as a church or mill, along a road or around a particular natural site such as a river or narrow valley. Some villages had no shape at all but seemed to be just an unattached group of dwellings.

Living Conditions

Left: The inside of a crofter's house in Shetland. Note that there is no roof insulation and only a small fire. A cottage such as this would have been extremely cold in winter.

Most village settlements are made up of houses of different ages, shapes, styles and building materials. This variety of buildings is useful as a guide for anyone who wishes to trace building development and styles through the ages.

All communities had social divisions, and this was clearly seen in the different types of buildings found within a village. The local landowner, the squire, the parson and a few other wealthy and important people usually lived in large, well-built houses. The people who worked on the land lived in houses that were paid for by the local landowner and built from materials that were cheap and easily available.

Village houses can provide historians with useful information about the changes in building methods and materials. Many houses were built before the Victorian age.

Look at them carefully because they show you how houses were built in times past. The basic house shape will have remained the same, and a few house will have their original windows and doors, but some will have changed as fashions changed.

Before Victorian times, many houses had been made from wood; only the wealthy could afford bricks or stone. However, by the 1880s, bricks were being mass-produced by machine and therefore much more plentiful and cheaper. This meant that almost all buildings from this period were built from brick.

Brick-built Victorian cottages in Bradfield.

Before the nineteenth century, many village houses had only one storey, and in the poorer homes, only one room. Even in Victorian times, some cottages built for farm labourers had no more than a single room downstairs, a kitchen under the stairs and a single bedroom upstairs. The type of room seen in the picture of the crofter's cottage (opposite page, top) would not have been uncommon in some English rural villages during the last century.

Labourers did not own their cottages but had to pay a small rent out of their wages. The rent of about 1 shilling (5p in today's money) a week may seem a very small sum, but remember, many labourers earned only about 7 shillings (35p) a week.

Pre-Victorian brick-making was carried out by hand.

The better-off workers in the community might have lived in a two-storey cottage with two rooms upstairs and two rooms downstairs. One of these would probably have been considered the 'best' room and furnished with the smartest pieces of furniture and treasured possessions. It would have been used only on Sundays or for very special occasions. A cottage of this size could have housed a large family! The facilities in these cottages were very basic. There was no electricity so all light came from candles. When cottagers could not afford candles they soaked rushes in bacon fat and burnt those. Later in the century, the people who could afford them used paraffin lamps. In most houses, cooking was done on a black cast-iron 'range' (cooker), which might have been the only source of heat. There was no central heating as we have in modern houses. The range would also contain an oven and a small hot-water tank.

Fresh water for daily use would have come either from a cast-iron pump above the stone sink in the kitchen or from the village pump. There were no inside toilets. People had to use earth 'privies' (toilets) in wooden or brick sheds at the bottom of the garden.

People in the middle- and upper-classes had better houses and more comfortable living conditions. Their houses would have contained many more rooms than a labourer's cottage, and the wealthy landowners would have had servants to look after the day-to-day running of the home. Maids did all the housework, cooks prepared the meals, and gardeners and under-gardeners looked after the grounds.

The kitchen range. All the meals would have been cooked on the range, which would also have provided the house with hot water.

We know from the 1891 census that Frederick Lewendon was gardener in one of the local 'big' houses. The census for Bradfield Hall tells us that the head of the family, Ann Connop, lived there with her daughter, two sons and four servants – cook, parlourmaid, housemaid and coachman.

We also know from the census that Thomas Usborne lived in Bradfield Lodge with his wife, three daughters, son, sister, nephew and niece. They were all looked after by a governess, nurse, parlourmaid, cook, housemaid, under-housemaid and coachman. All the servants except the coachman lived in the Lodge with the family, which gives us an idea of the size of the house!

Above: A water pump in a Victorian village. This would have been the only source of fresh water for many people.

Right: Bradfield Hall. Four members of the Connop family lived here in 1891 with four servants.

The Village Church

This is Tom Rowe with two of his children, Valentine and Catherine, standing outside the main gate of the parish church. Tom was the part-time grave digger and also a bell ringer.

Ask someone to think of a typical English village and he or she will probably mention a village green, a pub and a church. All were important in the life of a Victorian village. The parish church of St Andrew's in Bradfield was rebuilt in 1848 on a plot of land where there had been a church since the 1100s. The flint for the church walls was dug from a local site, which now has become an open Greek-style theatre. The rector and benefactor of the church, Thomas Stevens, rebuilt the church in memory of his parents. He found it very difficult to get enough parishioners to fill both the pews and the choir stalls, so he established Bradfield (St Andrew's) College close by in 1850 to increase church attendance.

In the very early part of the Victorian period, the local parson, or rector, was an important person in the village. Together with the local squire, or major landowner, he looked after many of the needs of the villagers, especially if they made their living by working on the squire's estate farm. However, the Victorian period saw an important change in the role of the church and clergy in village and town parishes.

Often the clergy were unpopular with the villagers. Some church rectors owned a great deal of land and had large estates employing many people. To make these pay, they introduced machinery on their farms and as a result many farm workers lost their jobs. Many rectors were Justices of the Peace (JPs) who sat in courts in the nearby towns. Because of their position, they often imposed laws about farming that the labourers did not like. As a result the clergy were sometimes seen to be on the side of the landowners.

As the Victorian period continued, the power the church had over the people in the parish weakened. Many people still attended church on the main religious festivals, but weekly attendance was not as high as it had once been. By the end of the period the local rector could no longer take for granted his high position in village life. He now had to earn the respect of his parishioners.

This is a Methodist chapel in the nearby village of Tutts Clump. On the side of the chapel there are two foundation stones which give the date when the church was built. The foundation stones are dated 1879.

Although many village churches are Anglican, there are many examples of Methodist and Nonconformist chapels that were built by people who did not wish to attend the parish church.

Rector Thomas Stevens rebuilt St Andrew's church and then founded St Andrew's College, now Bradfield College, to increase the number of people who would attend church services and sing in the choir.

This picture is taken from the same place as the picture on the page 16. You can see that little has changed over the past one hundred years.

This is a modern photo of the parish church in Bradfield. If you compare it with the Victorian photograph on page 16, you will see that very little has changed – the gate has gone and the yew bush has grown very big. The origin of the house on the right is unknown but is thought to have been used both as a lytch gate and as an ale house, where the coffin waited before entering the church and where the mourners could have a drink.

The parish church can be a very useful source of information for a historian. Somewhere on the walls you will usually find a list of previous vicars or rectors going back over centuries. The church had to be built in an area where there were enough people to attend services, so such a list will tell you when the settlement started to grow – although not the date when the present building was built. Some churches have been rebuilt many times, and the original building would be very difficult to find. Little remains of the original church in Bradfield. But since Victorian times, the inside of the church has remained virtually unchanged.

Right: Two tombstones in the church graveyard in memory of George Smith and his wife, Anne.

B482. Bradfield Church.

Above: The inside of St Andrew's church. The only changes since Victorian times are that the organ is sited on the left-hand side and the railings across the choir stalls have been removed.

Tombstones in the graveyard and church memorials provide useful information about people in the past. Victorian villagers were usually buried in the local churchyard, so it is possible to see entire families buried alongside each other or in the same plot. Some tombstones provide interesting details about families.

Further research into church records and census would provide historians with extra information. Tombstones like these shown in the picture on the left are a good starting point.

The Village School

Many villages had their own village school, like the one in the picture below, from the 1840s. Many schools started as Sunday Schools. They began to open during the week and were called National Schools. The idea of National Schools was to teach children to read the Bible. The school in Bradfield was built near the church and moved to its present site at Southend Bradfield in September 1886. When the school opened, there were three staff, a head teacher and ninety-five children. The school still has strong links with the church as shown by its name: Bradfield Church of England Primary School.

Village schools like Bradfield were very important because, for many children, they provided the only formal education they would have during their lifetime. We know a lot about village schools because of the log-book kept by each head teacher, in which he or she wrote all the events that had taken place each day. Log-books are now usually kept at the local Record Office. They provide us with a valuable record of school and village life.

In 1870, Parliament passed the Education Act, which stated that schools had to be provided for children between five and twelve years old. But many of the village children had other work to do.

A village school in the 1840s. One teacher is looking after a number of children. She keeps discipline with the use of a cane, but many of the children are not doing much learning!

Bradfield Church of England Primary School today. The outside of the school has changed little since it was built in 1886. The building with the blue doors was originally the head teacher's house. The extension on the left was opened in the 1960s.

These children worked on farms and preferred not to attend school. In 1880, an act was passed that made school compulsory for all children between the ages of five and ten. If children were caught missing school their parents could be fined. Those pupils who attended regularly were rewarded with prizes. However, school governors in rural areas such as Bradfield realized that children had to take on jobs in the community, so they often allowed children to take holidays to collect acorns or help with the harvest. The log-book said:

1884. 26 June. The haymaking having commenced several children were absent this week.

Many children, especially from isolated farms, had to travel a long way to get to school, sometimes 6-8 km, often over fields and muddy tracks. Their journeys were particularly difficult in bad weather and school attendance would drop.

1883. 5-7 March. Attendance much smaller than usual this week owing to very cold weather.

1885. 2 March. Wet weather. Attendance rather small.

1887. 15 March. Deep snow. Poor attendance.

The Victorians thought that the three Rs – Reading, wRiting and aRithmetic – were very important, and children spent part of each schoolday learning these subjects. The fourth R, Religion, was also considered to be very important especially in church schools, and pupils had Bible stories and assemblies almost every day.

Some lessons simply required the pupils to recite poems. Others were 'object' lessons in which children were expected to describe and perhaps paint a particular object.

Schools had few books, so the teacher put much of the information on the blackboard, and pupils copied it or learnt it by heart. Because paper was very expensive, many schools provided slates in wooden frames on which students could write with slate pencils.

Older children were allowed to use ink and 'dip pens'. A dip pen was simply a pen nib attached to a piece of wood. It made a scratchy sound and often left ink blots, which made the work untidy.

All pupils learned to write in the same style, called 'copperplate'. They were given a sentence at the top of a page or slate and would have to copy it out in the copperplate style. (The log-book, below, is printed in copperplate style.)

In some areas, children from the workhouse attended the local village school.

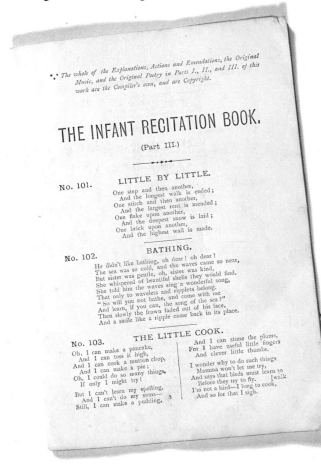

The first page of a recitation book for infants. Note how difficult some of the words are for the age group.

1885. 9 Feb.   The children from the Union Workhouse were admitted today and entered on the books. The number was 22.

1886. 15 Feb.   Admitted Christopher Stevens from the Union.

The log-book shows us other aspects of school and village life:

Discipline:

1889. 7 Jan.   F. Goodall punished this afternoon for playing truant.

The weather:

1888. 25 June.   Very heavy thunderstorm.

The festivals and entertainment taking place
in the village:

*1883. 14 Feb.   Small attendance today. Many
children went to Bradfield Hall for the
usual Valentine's Day Gift.*

*1883. 6 August.   Very small attendance today because
of Band-of-Hope tea party.*

*1888. 31 July.   Today was a holiday; it being
Bradfield Flower Show.*

*1886. 16 March.   Rev J Wallace gave a magic lantern show in the
large room this evening to which all the school children
were invited. Nearly 200 people were present.*

A slate and slate
pencil. Notice that
this one has lines
drawn on it to help
the children keep
their writing straight.

The attendance figures, the jobs pupils were expected to do
and the illnesses that some of the pupils had:

*1884. 25 Feb.   Received information that a case of smallpox had
occurred at Stanford and therefore the children from
that district would not be allowed to attend school.*

*1885. 7 Sept.   Outbreak of measles. By order of Dr Woodford the
school was closed until the infection had passed away.*

1885. 2 Nov.   The school reopened today (after 13 weeks.)

The log-books also give the results of tests and school
inspections. Of course they also provide the names of many of
the pupils, and this helps a historian trace a particular person
or family within a village.

The Victorian Workhouse

A young farm worker and his family. The poorest people would have to look to the workhouse for help in times of need.

Today, if people are unable to find work or they are too old or ill to get a job, they are usually given money by the government to help them buy food and pay their rent. This was not always the case. In Victorian times, people who could not work could not pay their rent. They could be thrown out of their houses and sent to the local workhouse. People who were widowed, orphaned or just too old to work could also end up in the workhouse.

Not all villages had workhouses. Some were in towns, so inmates came to them from a wide area. The Bradfield workhouse opened in 1835, at a cost of £4,500.

Workhouses were built in a similar style throughout the country. They were usually brick buildings with high walls and small windows, which gave them the look of a prison. Sometimes, as in Bradfield, the workhouse was built on a hill which made it even more uninviting. Nobody wanted to go to the workhouse, but if people were desperate and starving they had no other choice. The workhouse was paid for by the parish and controlled by a group of overseers.

In the workhouse, families were split up, and some never saw each other again. The building was divided up into three sections – for men, women and children. Babies over one year old were taken from their mothers and looked after in the children's area. In some workhouses, even the chapel had separate sections with separate entrances for men, women and children. At Bradfield there was a small church with no separate entrances. When inmates died, they were buried in the workhouse graveyard. Because they were poor, they had no headstones and were often buried three or four to a plot.

In some villages, people entered workhouses during those times of the year when the landowner could not employ them. There was often little work on a farm in the winter, so they would stay in the workhouse for a few weeks or months and then come out again during the spring and summer.

The front of the Bradfield Union in the 1890s. It looks rather like a large country house, but notice the small high windows, which gave little light into the inmates' dormitories.

Children outside a village school in Norfolk. The children are well dressed, but you can tell the workhouse children by their shaved heads.

Homeless people also used the workhouse overnight. They arrived at the opening time in the evening, usually 6 pm, gave up all their possessions, had a bath and were placed in a locked cell for the night. They were expected to work at breaking stones or other tasks, before they were allowed to go on their way.

Discipline was strict at the workhouse. There was no talking at mealtimes or during the work periods, and the food was always the same.

THE WORKHOUSE DIET

Breakfast	Dinner	Supper
6 oz [150 g] buttered bread 1 pint [0.6 l] of tea	4 oz [100 g] bacon 3 oz [75 g] of bread or potatoes	6 oz [150 g] bread 1 pint [0.6 l] of tea 2 oz [50 g] of cheese

The young children were given lessons for part of the day. Lessons were either in the workhouse school or in some villages at the local school. We know workhouse children attended the Bradfield school because of entries in the log-book:

1886. 11 March.   *Mr Perrin visited today to make enquiries about the attendance of the Union children.*

1886. 29 Oct.   *Admitted Alice Myles from the Union.*

Workhouse children who were old enough were sent to the local farms to work as cheap labour or into the towns to work in the new factories. Sometimes they were even sent abroad:

1887. 5 Sept.   *13 of the Union children have been sent out by the Guardians to Ottawa in North America.*

Workhouses closed in the 1930s. However, the buildings can still be seen in some areas today, although their use has changed. Many have become ordinary hospitals, some are centres for the disabled and others are old people's homes.

At one time, the Bradfield workhouse became a home for people with learning disabilities, known as the Wayland hospital, but it is now empty and crumbling.

You might like to find out if there was a workhouse in your area. If the buildings are still there, you may be able to go in and see evidence of male and female sections, the chapel and the graveyard. You may be able to find other evidence in your school's log-book of the Victorian period. Check to see if there are any references to 'union children' or 'children from the workhouse'.

The entrance to the Bradfield workhouse building, now the closed Wayland hospital, as it looks today.

Agricultural Workers

During Victorian times there were great changes in agriculture. This greatly affected the lives of the workers who had relied on traditional farm jobs to earn a living. Some farm labourers found themselves out of work because machines had taken over from them.

The horse-drawn plough was just beginning to be used for heavy ploughing, while the steam threshing machine was used at harvest time. It was now possible to get the crops gathered in within a few days rather than a few weeks.

A horse-drawn plough similar to those used on many Victorian farms. This one can be seen working on the Acton Scott Farming Museum in Shropshire.

A steam threshing machine. The traction engine on the right provided the power that drove the belt, which in turn powered the threshing machine.

The use of farm machinery meant that the labourers were not paid their usual harvest wages. Before steam power was used, some men were earning £6 to £8 for a few weeks' work, and the women also earned a few extra pennies by working in the fields during the harvest. With farming machines in use, the men were lucky to earn £3.

However, farm machines were very expensive, and only wealthy farmers or owners of large estates could afford them. Those with smaller farms still relied on men, women and even children to do most of the farm work. Children as young as seven and eight were employed to scare the crows from the corn fields, pick up stones, harvest potatoes and help their parents rake in the hay. For this they would have earned about a shilling (5p) a week.

During the Victorian period, many workers left the land and moved to the towns where they could find better paid jobs in the factories. Some moved to North America, Australia or New Zealand in search of work. For those who stayed behind working in the countryside, life was not very easy. Families often lived in poor, over-crowded housing and worked long hours for very low wages.

The average weekly wage for a labourer in the 1850s was 7 shillings (35p). Some labourers got an extra cider or milk allowance. Their usual diet was bread and potatoes with seasonal vegetables grown in the garden. The few kitchen scraps were sometimes fed to a pig, which was fattened up during the year then killed and salted in the autumn to provide meat for the winter months. Some of the meat was sold to raise money to buy a piglet for the next year. Those families who did not have a pig of their own fed scraps to a neighbour's pig in return for a share of the meat.

Fuel was expensive but necessary for cooking and heating. Timber could be

Raking in the hay. This was a job that even the children could help with.

collected from the woods with the owner's permission, but other fuels such as coal – and in some areas, peat – had to be bought when it was required.

A typical weekly shopping list for a labourer in the 1850s:

Bread	Potatoes	Bacon	Salt	Tea	Soap	Candles	Coal	Peat
5 loaves	3 pecks *	½ lb		¼ oz	5 lb	¼ lb	½ cwt *	1 d
2s 6d	1s 6d	3½ d	¼ d	1d	3d	1½ d	5d	1d
(12½ p)	(7½ p)	(1½ p)		(½ p)	(1½ p)	(¾ p)	(2½ p)	(½ p)

Rent   1s 6d (7½ p)

Total 6s 9¼ d (34¾ p)

* [1 peck = 8 quarts/13½ litres of dry measure]

* [1 cwt = a hundredweight or 112 lb]

(*Source:* Victorian Somerset. John Hodges a Farm Labourer *by A. Heely and M. Brown*)

Clothes were a luxury and were mended and adapted until they wore out completely. The costs might work out as follows:

Clothes	Cost	Clothes	Cost
Farmer's smock	2s 6d (12½p)	Shirt	1s (5p)
Boots	5s (25p)	Stockings (per pair)	6d (2½p)
Second-hand waistcoat	6d (2½p)	Woman's cloak (second-hand)	1s 3d (6½p)
Coat	1s 6d (7½p)	Skirt	8d (3½p)
Trousers	1s (5p)	Shoes (per pair)	1s 6d (7½p)

(*Source:* Victorian Somerset. John Hodges a Farm Labourer *by A. Heely and M. Brown*)

A few houses in Bradfield were supplied with gas. Bradfield was one of the first villages in the country to have a gas works.

Imagine what life would have been like for farm labourer and villager George Titchener. He would earn money only while he was working. If it rained too hard, he would be sent home with no pay. If workers were ill, they did not get paid unless they were a member of a 'friendly society'. This was a type of insurance company that provided money for members who became ill; it also paid for their funerals when they died. Members of the friendly society paid a sum of money, perhaps 4 shillings (20p), every quarter of the year. For this they received sick pay if they needed it. Those members who had a serious illness and were not able to work at all could be sent to the workhouse together with their family.

Some women – for example, Susannah Titchener, George's wife – took in washing and did other jobs to make some extra money or provide a basic income so that they could stay in their cottages.

An artist's idea of the inside of a farm labourer's cottage in 1872.

Occupations

Victorian villagers rarely left the home villages they lived in. Everything they wanted to buy could be found in the village. If you look at the list of occupations from the 1891 census in the Appendix on page 43 you will see the jobs and trades of the villagers. Among them are trades that we would find unusual today – for example, a mineral-waterman and soda-water bottler. The waterman was also listed as a 'fly' owner (a 'fly' was a small horse-drawn carriage, which people could hire in the same way as a modern taxi).

Out of 1,036 people who lived in the village, 145 were classed as labourers, 48 were servants, and 177 were listed as scholars or children of school age.

In Bradfield, there were three people who were grocers and bakers, including Albert Chapman. Compare the Victorian picture (below) with the modern picture.

The number of servants shows us that there were large houses in the village and enough employers who could pay the servants' wages. The census also tells us the names of people who worked in service and the houses where they worked: such as the house-boys (who did the chores), kitchenmaids, housemaids, parlourmaids, butlers and housekeepers who worked at big houses like Bradfield Hall and Bradfield Lodge.

Coachmen, grooms, stableboys, gardeners, gamekeepers and under-keepers (who made sure that the owner of the house had a pheasant to shoot during the shooting season) were also employed.

Above: The blacksmith's shop at the Vulcan Arms in a small Welsh village. The blacksmith was a very important person at a time when horses were the main source of transport and power on the farms.

Left: A Victorian milkman delivering milk in a Dorset village. The buckets of milk were suspended on a yoke that went over his shoulders.

Some of the servants were very young, such as George Wingrove aged thirteen, a house-boy, and John Allen, aged fourteen who was a footman. Over one hundred people relied on the big houses for employment. We could also add to the list the governesses, who educated

Left: Bradfield is still a farming community. This photograph shows Southend Farm in Victorian times.

the children of the house before they went to school and the nurses, nursemaids and nursegirls who looked after their well-being.

The list also tells us that Bradfield is in a rural and farming area. Listed in the census were 18 farmers in the village and 3 farm bailiffs (who managed farms for other people). One hundred and forty five people, or 14 per cent of the population, were recorded as being labourers or agricultural labourers. So, even with the growth of machinery it seems that lots of men, women and children were still needed to do the many tasks on the farm.

Many rural villages had their own mill to grind the corn. Some, as in Bradfield, were water powered. Others, like this one shown here from Acle in Norfolk, were wind-powered.

34

The census also listed occupations such as dairymen, shepherds and cowmen, which shows that there were other jobs in agriculture such as the farming of animals. Some other occupations listed indicate that times were changing. Electricity and gas were new sources of power, especially in country areas, and there was one electrical engineer and one gas man living in the village.

Census details from villages in different areas of the country would give evidence of the major occupations such as mining or fishing that provided most of the jobs for the community. The information also gives historians a clue to the problems that would occur in such areas if a mine closed or the farmers began to rely heavily on machinery or the fishing grounds no longer provided enough fish to make a living. If for example, a mine closed, the men and women who worked in the mines or related trades would be out of work. They would have no money to spend, so the village shops and other traders would also lose money and might have to move to the nearest town to make a living.

Photographs can provide clues as to the location of a settlement. These villagers are selling fish outside their cottages in Cromarty, Scotland. We can assume that this village is near the coast and these people made their living from the sea.

Communications

This type of pony and trap would have been seen in many Victorian villages and towns.

The Victorian period saw many changes in transport and communications. The canals, once a major transport network, were no longer widely used except for goods that could be transported slowly. The condition of the main roads became much better throughout the century, but journeys still took a long time. However, from the early 1840s the growth of railways had a dramatic effect on the lives of many people. Food could be delivered more quickly, so it arrived much fresher. Newspapers were available every day. Cheap transport helped industries to grow, and the rail network meant that people could live out of the cities but travel daily to work. They could even go on holidays by train.

Rail travel made life easier for people who lived in towns and cities or even in villages with a rail link, but not for people who lived far away from railway stations or main roads. Roads in the countryside were not as good as the major routes. They were often rutted by heavy farm carts, and many country roads could not be used in the winter.

There was usually no country horse-coach service or any other form of public transport. Safety bicycles were not developed until 1885, and just a few cars appeared in cities the same year. Most villagers had to walk to wherever they needed to go, or make their way to the nearest train station or major road, which could have been many kilometres away. Village people did not have easy access to the new goods that could be found in the shops in the towns.

Although Bradfield was fairly isolated, it was almost self-sufficient. Most day-to-day goods could be found in Bradfield itself. If you look at the census for 1891, you will see there were four grocers, four bakers (plus three people who were both grocers and bakers). The village also had two tailors. Many villages also had their own butcher.

The old butcher's shop in Southend Bradfield is today a house.

A butcher's shop in Surrey. The butcher obviously liked plants, judging by the number of pots above the front door!

Larger items such as furniture, rolls of cloth or clothes were usually only available in towns that had department stores, which sold a wide range of goods. Villagers with their own transport, such as a coach traps, farm carts or horses, travelled into the town, usually on market day. At the market, villagers and townspeople could buy provisions and even sell some of their own goods. Those without transport could ask the village carrier to do their shopping for them for a small charge. Customers would give the carrier a shopping list and the money to go into town to buy their goods, which he would deliver in the evening. With this service available there was no need for people to leave the village if they did not wish to.

Some traders from the nearby towns often visited the outlying villages and sold their goods from the back of a cart or from a stall in the village hall. They knew the best times to visit – for instance, some tailors used to travel around the farms and villages at harvest time when the agricultural labourers had more money in their pockets and might be tempted to buy a new suit.

Market day. Some towns had one or more markets a week when many people would come in from the surrounding area to buy and sell goods.

This trader is collecting poultry from rural homes and taking them to market.

By the turn of the century transport to the towns was becoming easier, and many craftspeople in the villages had to compete with the variety and lower costs of the goods in the town shops. Many of the traditional trades gradually died out, and some villages were left with only one or two tradespeople offering the basic requirements.

Bradfield now has only one grocer's shop and the Post Office; it no longer has a bakery or a tailor's shop. However, during the summer months it does have its own regular Saturday morning market where villagers can buy and sell locally produced or home-made products, so, in a small way, the village continues to enjoy some of the self-sufficiency of previous times.

This is a carrier on his rounds at Sibford Ferris near Banbury, Oxfordshire, in 1874. These carriers often had regular 'visiting' days when villagers knew they could order goods to be collected from the town.

Appendix

CENSUS

Administrative county of Berks
Civic Parish Bradfield

Road or street name	Name and Surname	Relation to head of family	Age	Profession or occupation	Where born
1. Southend Road	Fraser Guyatt	Head	57	Register of births and deaths	Englefield, Berks
	Emma Guyatt	Wife	37		London, St Georges
2. Do.	Christina Potter	Wife	34	Draper	Walsall, Staffs
	Emma M. Do.	Daughter	5		Warwickshire, Beasely
	Henry J. Do.	Son	3		Berks, Bradfield
	Joseph R. Do.	Son	2		Do.
	Alma M. Do.	Daughter	3 mo		Do.
	John Do.	Nephew	15	Draper's assistant	Worcs. Shepston
3. Do.	George Millson	Head; widower	45	Bricklayer	Berks. Stanford Dingley
	Alice J. Do.	Daughter	17	Housekeeper	Do.
	Ellen L Do.	Daughter	15		Do.
	George J. Do.	Son	14	Farm labourer	Do.
	Sarah A. Do.	Daughter	12	Scholar	Do.
	Lizzie E. Do.	Daughter	10	Scholar	Do.
	Ruth L. Do.	Daughter	3		Do.
	Esther M. Do	Daughter	3		Do.
4. Do.	Amy Hall. Do.	Wife	29	Wife of Hotel Waiter	Bucklebury
	Flora L. Do.	Daughter	6		Surrey. Guildford
	Dorcas. Do.	Daughter	3		Berks. Bradfield
	Emily. Do.	Daughter	1		Do.
5. Do	George Wheeler	Head	41	Farm Labourer	Do.
	Emma Wheeler	Wife	42		Do.
	George E.	Son	16	Farm Labourer	Do.
	Enos Do.	Son	14	Do.	Do.
	Jessie Do.	Daughter	10	Scholar	Do.
	Bertha Do.	Daughter	8		Do.
	Edward Do.	Son	3		Do.
6. Lodge	Frederick Hall	Head	30	Groom in thoroughbred stud	Herefordshire, Welsh Newton
	Annie Hall	Wife	28		Berks, Tilehurst
	Winifred Do.	Daughter	5		Berks, Bradfield
	Leonard Do.	Son	2		Do.

OCCUPATIONS

Trade
Bricklayer (2)
Draper (2)
Carrier/Coal Merchant (5)
Gas Man (1)
Builder (1)
Needlewoman (1)
Carpenter/Joiner (12)
Broom Maker (1)
Baker/Grocer (9)
Grocer's Assistant (2)
Tanner (2)
Decorator (2)
Dressmaker (1)
Innkeeper (4)
Blacksmith (5)
Bootmaker (4)
Tailor (1)
Tailor's Apprentice (1)
Wheelwright (1)

General
Labourer (69)
Capt. Royal Artillery (1)
Army Pensioner (1)
Pedlar & Hawker (2)
Soda Water Bottler (1)
Engine Fitter (1)
Postmaster (1)
Postal Clerk (1)
Postman (1)
Police Constable (1)

Mineral Waterman & Fly Owner (1)
Engineer in Steam Laundry (1)
Stationary Engine Driver (1)

Agriculture
Labourer (76)
Watercress Grower (2)
Market Gardener (2)
Hay Dealer (1)
Milk Boy (1)
Stable Boy (1)
Fruit Grower (1)
Dairyman (3)
Dairywoman (1)
Farm Bailiff (3)
Shepherd (4)
Cowman (3)
Farmers (18)
Farm Boy (2)
Carter (10)

Education
Scholar (177)
Schoolmaster (2)
Teacher (3)
Maths Student (1)

Professional
Physician (1)
Registrar (1)
Surveyor (1)
Electrical Engineer (1)
Parish Clerk (1)

Rector (1)
Methodist Minister (1)
Barrister (1)
Midwife (1)

Domestic
Servants (48)
Housekeeper (8)
Groom (4)
Gardener (13)
Laundress (17)
Washer Woman (1)
Mother's Help (2)
Charwoman (2)
Butler (3)
Housemaid (5)
Kitchenmaid (1)
Coachman (6)
Footman (3)
Governess (5)
Nurse (3)
Nursegirl (1)
Nursemaid (2)
Parlourmaid (2)
Cook (4)
Under-Domestic (1)
House-boy (1)

Estate
Gamekeeper (4)
Under Keeper (1)
Land Agent (1)
Woodman (2)

Map of Bradfield

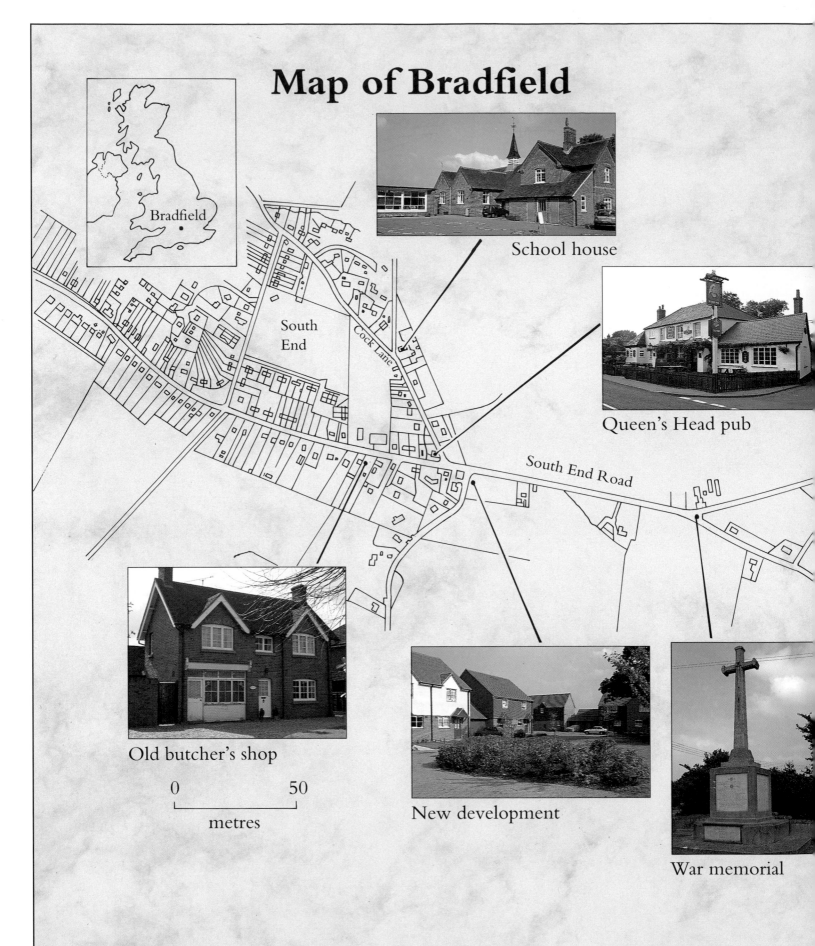

Bradfield

School house

Queen's Head pub

South End

Cock Lane

South End Road

Old butcher's shop

0   50

metres

New development

War memorial

Church

Mill stream

River Pang

Bradfield

Union Road

The workhouse

Greek theatre

Timeline

The Bradfield entries are shown in green.

1830s

1834 New Poor Law came into being. Many workhouses built.

1835 Bradfield workhouse opened.

1837 Victoria came to the throne.

1850s

1843 The first Christmas card was sent.

1846 Pupil-teacher system started in schools.

1848 St. Andrew's church was built in Bradfield.

1848 The Public Health Act aimed to improve sanitary conditions.

1850 The Great Exhibition in London displayed inventions and goods.

1860s

1861 Mrs Beeton's *Book of Household Management* published.

1862 'Payment by results' introduced for teachers. Log-books to be kept by elementary school heads.

1866 Dr Elizabeth Garrett became the first woman doctor in Britain.

1866 First Dr Barnardo's home opened.

1874 Post-boxes painted red.

1876 The telephone was invented by Alexander Graham Bell.

1878 William Booth founded the Salvation Army.

1879 Methodist chapel opened in the village of Tutt's Clump.

1885 Karl Benz drove a petrol-powered car.

1885 The first 'safety bicycle' was invented by Rover.

1885 Workhouse children attended school for the first time.

1885 New classroom was built in the village school.

1885 School was closed for thirteen weeks because of a measles epidemic.

1895 Object lessons made compulsory for all infants.

1896 'Red flag' Act repealed. A flag no longer needed to be carried in front of a car.

Speed limit raised to 20 kph on roads.

1897 National Union of Women's Suffrage Societies formed to co-ordinate the campaign to get women the vote.

1899 Compulsory education for all children up to twelve years old.

1899 The Boer War.

1840s

1837 Telegraph invented by Samuel Morse.	1840 Penny Post invented by Rowland Hill.		1842 Coal Mines Act stopped children from working underground.	1842 Queen Victoria first travelled on a train.
1850 Bradfield College opened.	1851 A census showed that 40 per cent of people attended church or chapel.	1854–6 The Crimea War. Florence Nightingale improved hospital conditions.	1856 Henry Bessemer's steel converter invented.	1859 Charles Darwin wrote *The Origin of Species*.

1870s

1868 Trades Union Congress established.	1870 Forster's Education Act introduced the state education system. It allowed school boards to set up Board Schools.	1872 Agricultural Labourers' Union formed to improve wages for farm workers.	1872 Bank holidays introduced.	1872 Scottish Education Act passed.

1880s

1880 Mundella's Act. Schooling compulsory to the age of ten.	1884 Gottlieb Daimler rode a motorcycle with a petrol engine.	1884 Farm labourers get the vote.	1884 Outbreak of smallpox in neighbouring village meant that children could not attend school.	1884 The school buildings were bought by Dr Watney.

1890s

1886 Villagers voted to keep the Church school rather than a Board School.	1886 School moved to a new site in Southend Bradfield. Officially opened in October.	1887 Queen's Jubilee. School treat with tea, sports and fireworks.	1888 John Dunlop invented the pneumatic tyre.	1892 A large detachment of Cavalry passed through the village.

1900s

1900 The Independent Labour Party formed.	1901 Queen Victoria died.	1902 Balfour's Education Act. Local Education Authorities to run a free, national system of schools.	1908 Old age pensions started for people over seventy.	1909 The first Woolworths store opened in Britain.

Glossary

Anglican
The Church of England.

Bailiff
A landowner's agent who manages a farm or estate for the owner.

Census
The official count of the population. In Britain a census is taken every ten years.

Coach trap
A closed carriage with two wheels.

Compulsory
Must be done; required.

Crofter
A person who rents a smallholding.

Inmate
A person who lives in an institution.

Justice of the Peace (JP)
An unpaid magistrate who hears minor cases in court.

Lytch gate
An elaborate gate leading to a church.

Methodist
A Christian Church founded in the eighteenth century by John and Charles Wesley.

Nonconformist
A Christian Church that separated from the Church of England.

Parish
The area served by a church.

Parson
A clergyman in charge of a parish.

Safety bicycle
The first modern bicycle with a toothed gear wheel and a chain to the back wheel.

Squire
A country gentleman, usually the major landowner in an area.

Threshing machine
A farm machine for separating the grain from the chaff.

Vicar
A parish priest in the Church of England.

Further Information

Books to read

There are many books about the Victorian countryside, and some may be about your own area. You can find these in the 'local interest' section of your local bookshop.

Some of the books listed below are quite old, but they should be available in your library. You may have to ask the librarian to find them for you.

Books for children:

Brown, J. and Ward, S. *The Village Shop* (Rural Development Committee, 1983)
Chamberlain, E. R. *Victorians and their Times* (Beehive Books, 1993)
Wood, R. *A Victorian School* and *A Victorian Street* (Wayland, 1993)

Photo collections about rural life:

Winter, G. *A Country Camera 1844–1914* (David and Charles, 1966)
Brown, J. and Ward, S. *Village Life in England 1860–1940* (Batsford, 1985)

Other books:

These adult books have been chosen because they contain information that may help you in a local study.

Brown, J. *Farm Machinery 1750–1945* (Batsford, 1989)
Fletcher, R. (ed) *A Biography of a Victorian Village* (Batsford, 1977)
(This book is Richard Cobbold's account of the village of Wortham in Sussex in 1860)
Horn, P. *The Victorian Country Child* (Roundwood Press, 1974)
Longmate, N. *The Workhouse* (Temple Smith, 1974)
Mingay, G.E. (ed). *The Victorian Countryside vols I and II* (Routledge & Kegan Paul, 1981)
Mingay G.E. (ed). *The Village Labourer* by J. & B. Hammond (Longman, 1978)
Morgan, D. *Harvesters and Harvesting 1840–1900* (Croon Helm, 1982)
Philip, N. *Victorian Village Life* (Albion, 1993)

To help you develop the skills to organize and write a local study see *Foundation Skills History, vols I, II and III* by M.L. Parsons (Letts, 1986)

Places to visit

There are many folk and farming museums around the country, so it would be worth looking them up in the telephone directory or contacting your local museum to see if there are any in your area.

Index

Numbers that appear in **bold** refer to the pictures.